The Widow Who **Got Scammed**

by Davin Martin

Fraud AWARE

Fraud AWARE

Phone or Text: (717) 740-2790
Email: info@FraudAware.us
Website: www.FraudAware.us

ISBN: 979-8-9915815-0-9

Printed in USA

FIRST EDITION – First Printing, September 2024
FIRST EDITION – Second Printing, October 2024

The content provided herein is for informational purposes only, provided merely to raise awareness of some of the potential ways that fraud can arise in any community. Nothing herein should be construed as legal, tax, investment, financial, or other advice. None of the information or examples provided herein depict or describe any real persons or events.

Order additional copies from:

CHRISTIAN LIGHT PUBLICATIONS

Website: christianlight.org
Phone: 800-776-0478
Fax: 540-433-8896
Mail: PO Box 1212
Harrisonburg, VA 22803
Email: orders@christianlight.org

Discount available for bookstores.

Table of Contents

The most successful thieves may not carry guns, hide their faces behind ski masks, or break into your house.

They just might steal your money while sitting in an easy chair, sipping lemonade, and talking to you on the phone.

SALE
%
$
24

They use the weapons of fear, lies, and your gullibility to convince you to give them a free shopping spree. These thieves are usually known as scammers.

In 2023, Americans reported over $10 billion[1] lost to scams! That's over $19,000 in the minute since you started reading this book, and that doesn't even include ***unreported*** losses!

Here's one of the ways it could happen to you!

The Widow Who Got Scammed

For Tara, Ralph, and Bob, it was another day of work.

For Sarah Weaver, it was a nightmare.

The Widow Who Got Scammed

Sarah was knitting one day when an out-of-state number called. "Hello, this is Sarah!" she answered.

"Hello, Sarah Weaver. This is Charlotte Blink from the North Hills FBI Drug Force Investigative Office, Employee ID TB343910. I'm sorry to inform you that an international drug gang is using your name and address to smuggle drugs. Would you have time to answer a few questions?"

Scammer Weapon Alert

Scammers lie as easily as many people tell the truth.

"What? Me? What did you say about drug gangs?" Sarah stammered.

"I'm so sorry. I'm sure we can get this cleared up. Let me transfer you to the lead investigator. Please hold," Tara said while stifling a giggle.

Delighted to have finally made contact, Tara roused Ralph from a doze. "We've got another victim on the line! She sounds scared!"

FBI

Ralph snapped awake, all business. "I've got it, Tara! Bob, are you ready for her when I'm done?"

"Yes, sir!" Bob replied.

Ralph picked up the line. "Agent Smithrock, North Hills FBI Drug Force Investigative Office, Badge Number US 3493, speaking. Could you please confirm your name and birthdate?"

Sarah hesitated, then said, "Sarah Weaver, birthdate of 10/01/1948."

Scammer Weapon Alert

Scammers use professional sounding terms to gain your trust.

Smiling, Tara typed the information, winking at Ralph who continued quickly, "Thank you, that matches our records. As our outreach officer informed you, this serious matter demands your immediate cooperation. An international drug gang inserted illegal drugs into a package addressed to you. Criminals in your area are monitoring your porch to pick up the package before you get it. Can we confirm your address, so we know if they have your correct address or not?"

Sarah hesitated,

Shouldn't a federal government agency know my address?

"123 Dry Spring Road, Dry Spring, PA 17435."

Scammer Weapon Alert

Scammers talk fast to confuse you.

Ralph gasped, "Oh no, Sarah, that is the address on the package. They probably know all your personal information and are preparing to drain your bank accounts. Listen, Sarah, this drug ring doesn't mess around. They are under investigation by the United States, Mexico, and the United Kingdom. Have you noticed any unusual activity outside your home today?"

"No, I haven't." Sarah responded, rising to lock her doors. "When might they be coming?"

Scammer Weapon Alert

Scammers use fear to override your common sense.

"Most likely not until the package is supposed to arrive. Remember these are armed and dangerous drug gangs. We are ready to arrest close to one hundred criminals, and with your complete cooperation, we may catch even more. This may sound strange, but do not tell your local police. If they find the package, they may arrest you. We are deploying an FBI officer to your neighborhood to collect information and to respond if your safety is at risk.

"I will also begin working with you to move your money to a secure account until the investigation is done. Is anyone home with you?"

Scammer Weapon Alert

Scammers make you distrust the people you should trust.

"No," Sarah responded, "but my daughter might soon stop in. Should I warn her?"

Tara smothered a laugh as Ralph intoned, "No, no, no! Do not tell her! That'll get her in trouble. You likely do not need to fear physical harm, but we will keep our call connected so we can provide immediate help."

Sarah's mind swirled. *What is going on? Maybe I should call someone to ask for advice. But whom, and what if they call the police? Imagine what people would think if a grandmother like me is arrested on drug charges. I'd get my picture on the front page of the newspaper!*

"Okay, thanks. Now, let's confirm your Social Security number," Ralph said firmly.

Sarah paused. *This has to be a scam. I should just hang up!* Instead of hanging up, she asked, "Officer Smithrock, how do I know you are not a scammer?"

"Of course I'm not a scammer. How can I help you if you don't trust me? Time is running out, and you need to cooperate, or we'll lose our opportunity to help you. Would you like to talk to my manager?" Sarah agreed, and Ralph placed the call on hold. Just then a delivery van stopped outside, and the driver jumped out. Sarah's heart froze. *Was the package here? Were the gangs far behind?*

The man ran to her neighbor's house, delivered the package, and took off. Sarah ran upstairs, hands sweating, peering at the box on her neighbor's porch.

When would the manager ever answer?

Scammer Weapon Alert

Scammers create a sense of urgency to confuse your thinking.

Bob soon picked up. "Good morning. Officer York with North Hills FBI Drug Force Investigative Office speaking. Is this Sarah Weaver?"

"Yes," Sarah replied.

"Ms. Weaver, I know this is frightening, but you need to cooperate better with us. We are going out of our way to protect you. These drug gangs are nothing to mess with. The clock is ticking, and we are very limited in who we can help. If you don't cooperate with us, we may decide our time is better spent helping others. May I transfer you back to Agent Smithrock?"

Scammer Weapon Alert

Scammers shame you for asking valid questions.

When she agreed, Bob placed her on hold. Sarah blushed. *How could I be so ungrateful? I just wasted their time and made their job more difficult.* A few minutes ticked by. *What if Officer Smithrock doesn't pick up? Why is he taking so long?*

Bob grinned as Ralph and Tara flashed a thumbs-up at him. "She's all yours, Officer Smithrock. More cash is coming soon!"

"Not too fast," Ralph responded. "If we make her sweat it out a little more, she will be more compliant." After two minutes, he picked up Sarah's call.

"Agent Smithrock speaking. Did you get your confirmation, Sarah?"

"Yes, I'm sorry for wasting your time. What do I need to do?"

Ralph was ready, "Well, that's okay. I understand someone asking for confirmation. As a matter of fact, it tells me that you are too smart to get ripped off by scammers. Trust me, these drug gangs and scammers make me so angry, but that's why I've dedicated my life to fighting crime. Now, may I have your Social Security number?"

Scammer Weapon Alert

Scammers trap you with flattery.

SOCIAL SECURITY
XX3-45-6789
THIS NUMBER HAS BEEN ESTABLISHED FOR
SARAH WEAVER
Sarah Weaver
SIGNATURE
USA

Sarah hesitated. *If they are with the government, why don't they know my Social Security number?* Then she remembered that she had already taken too much of their time and needed to cooperate better, so she gave it.

"Thanks," Ralph said, "Next we need your husband's Social Security number and date of birth."

WEAVER

"My husband died five years ago," Sarah said, puzzled they didn't know that.

Ralph quickly jumped in, "I'm so sorry to hear that. Yes, we did know that," lied Ralph, "but we still need to confirm our records."

Bob mouthed to Tara, "What good luck! We got a widow!"

Ralph continued, "Let me repeat. You play a critical role in helping us arrest as many gang members as possible. In addition, your safety and our ability to prove your innocence rest on you keeping this quiet for a short 48-hour time period. Understand?"

Sarah agreed.

"Good. Now we should move your money to our secure accounts. Would you like us to help you with that?"

"Yes, please do."

"You need to go to the bank, withdraw about $10,000, and then buy gift cards. Buy no more than $2,500

Scammer Weapon Alert

Scammers often pose as people helpers.

at each store. We have found that JewelryOnline and SuperStore Online cards do not trigger fraud alerts.

"If we get disconnected, please call back immediately. Keep your phone in your pocket so we can hear what's going on and send rescue agents if necessary. When you get out of the store, we will give you further instructions. Remember, act as if nothing is wrong. If you are questioned about withdrawing money, tell them you are giving someone a gift. If you see a police officer, simply look away or smile.

Do you have any questions?"

"No," Sarah said.

Scammer Weapon Alert

Scammers pressure you not to tell others.

"Okay, then let's get started securing your money. If you need any help, just ask. We will mute ourselves, but as soon as you ask us a question, we will respond." Ralph muted his phone, leaned back in his chair, and began discussing with Tara what food they wanted to order into the office that evening. Since they were several time zones away from Sarah, they'd have to be up late.

Scammer Weapon Alert

Scammers require you to keep the phone connected.

As Sarah drove to the bank, her mind raced with worry. *What if the police freeze my bank accounts? What if I endanger my children or grandchildren? Is that the FBI or a drug gang following me in that blacked-out pickup?* She pulled up to the ATM, inserted her card, and tried to withdraw $10,000. A message flashed, "To combat fraud, withdrawals of this size must be processed inside." She parked as close to the door as possible, then hurried inside.

"How are you today?" the teller asked.

Fraud Prevention Fact

It is unwise to ignore warnings; they are given for a reason.

"Oh, all right. I just need some cash for something that came up," Sarah stammered, handing over the withdrawal slip. *Am I looking calm? Is Officer Smithrock still listening?*

"Well, $10,000 cash is a lot of money. Just be aware that there are a lot of scams going on."

"Well, it's for..." Sarah caught herself as she remembered that Agent Smithrock was listening, "it's for an emergency." Sarah took her money and almost ran out the door. This was only the first of several withdrawals she would have to make today.

Fraud Prevention Fact

If the bank teller asks a question, tell them what you are doing. They are trained to detect fraud!

Purchasing the gifts cards was easier. She entered the store, found the JewelryOnline gift cards, and grabbed five. The cashier scanned the cards, curiously inspecting this Mennonite grandmother buying gift cards for a jewelry store, and said, "I wonder who the lucky granddaughter is who's getting this for Christmas. Just remember, gift cards are for gifts, not paying bills."

When Sarah silently stared back, the cashier finished up as fast as possible.

Sarah walked to the adjoining store and bought five $500 gift cards for SuperStore Online.

Fraud Prevention Fact

Listen to advice from people you know and trust.

Relieved to be back in her car, Sarah drove to the far corner of the parking lot. “Officer Smithrock, are you still there?”

“Absolutely, Sarah. You did a fantastic job. Most people make a bad situation worse by losing their heads. Yes, it’s such a pity what these drug gangs are doing to victims like you. Now, when you read the codes we will transfer the money to a secure account. When the transaction clears, we will give you a confirmation code. These codes are the keys which will guarantee you get your money back. Okay, we’re ready.”

Fraud Prevention Fact

Gift cards are for gifts, not for transferring funds!

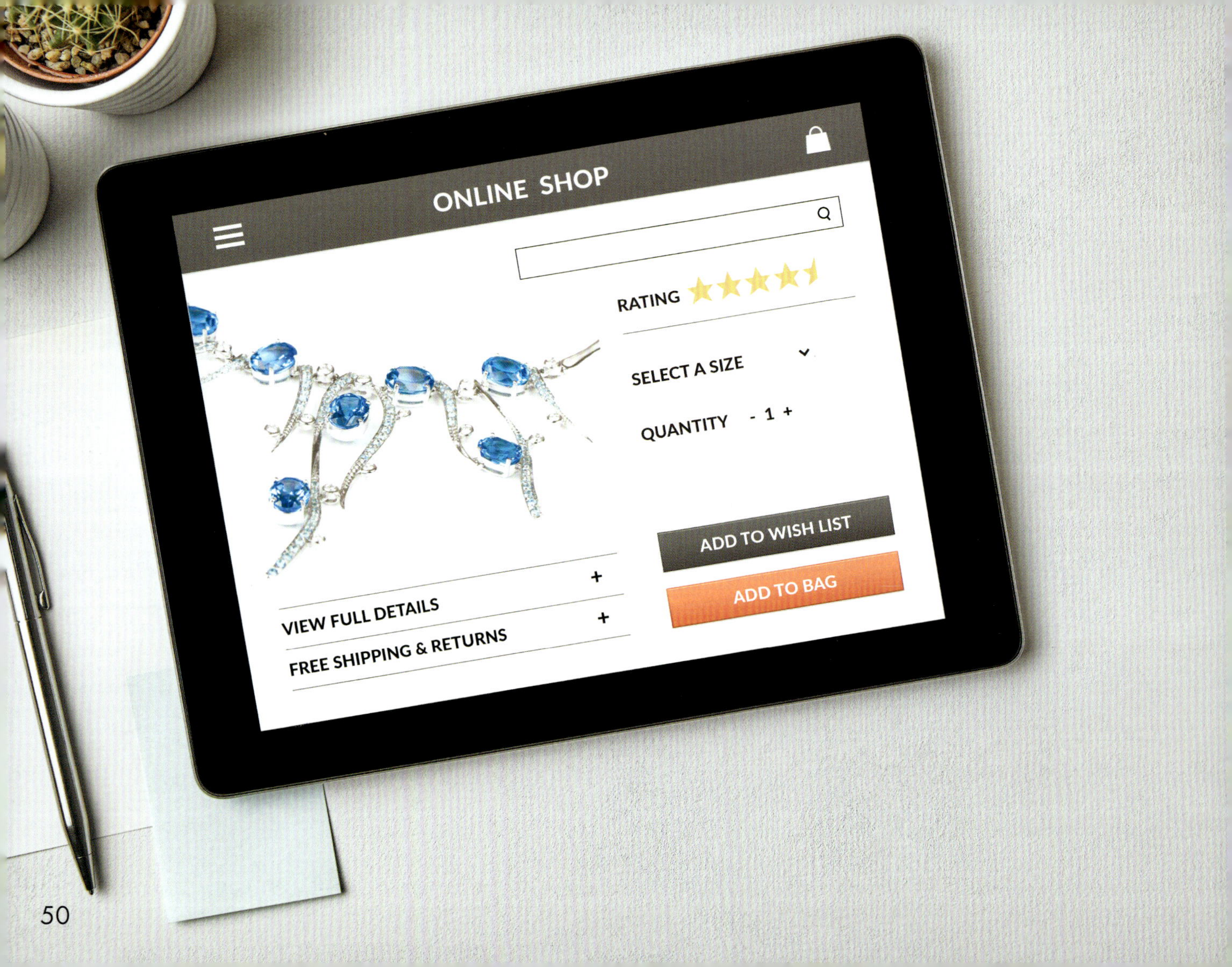
ONLINE SHOP
RATING
SELECT A SIZE
QUANTITY - 1 +
ADD TO WISH LIST
ADD TO BAG
VIEW FULL DETAILS +
FREE SHIPPING & RETURNS +

Sarah began, "I9Z32SEK898." As Ralph repeated it, Tara double-checked the numbers, and Bob entered it into the JewelryOnline web store. In a few seconds, a message posted on Bob's computer, "$500 gift card applied to your purchase." Bob flashed a thumbs-up. Ralph winked and gave Sarah a fake confirmation code.

"Very good, Ms. Weaver. Next?"

Sarah was relieved to know that her first $500 was safe. She read the next code, "19B78SGG328." Within minutes, Bob used the JewelryOnline gift cards to buy a blue sapphire and diamond necklace.

Ralph continued, "Great. Now let's secure the funds on the SuperStore Online cards."

Sarah's eyes hurt from reading the fine print. On the card, she noticed a message: "**Fraud Warning:** This card is a gift for you. Do not repeat this code over the phone to make a payment!" *What should she do? If the package arrived before she got the code across the phone, she would lose her money.* She started reading the codes which Tara used to purchase a widescreen TV.

"Excellent, excellent! Now did you receive any fraud alerts or notice any police or gang members giving you unusual attention?" Ralph asked Sarah.

"No."

"Good. We've got the first $5,000 secured, but I believe you said you had withdrawn $10,000. Let's get the rest of the money safe, and then we'll do another bank withdrawal. I'll mute until you're ready. All right?" asked Ralph.

"Sounds good!" Sarah said.

What She Thought
What Actually Happened
$500,000 BONUS
WIN UP TO $500,000!
OVER 15 CHANCES TO WIN!
FAST $50
MICHIGAN LOTTERY
Did I Win?

Meanwhile, Bob had just won approval for a new credit card in Sarah's name. He had to play it right. As long as he made small purchases spaced out right, the credit card fraud prevention wouldn't shut him down. *Important things first,* he thought as he purchased one hundred Big Billions lottery tickets.

As Sarah drove to the next store, she thought, *This won't be so bad after all. A few more hours of this, and my money will be safe. Thankfully, this will all be over after Friday when the big drug arrests will be made.*

Scam Story Observations

Agent Smithrock
Drug Package
Drug Gangs
HANG UP!

Scam Story Observations

Sarah could have ended her nightmare by simply hanging up.

- There were no drugs inserted into a package addressed to her.
- There was no Agent Smithrock or Officer York.
- There were no drug gangs waiting to pick up a package on her porch.
- There were only fear and lies—

and the best response to fear and lies is the truth.[2]

You Can Hang UP!
Gift cards are
for gifts, NOT
for payments.

The truth is . . .

- You can hang up at any time!
- Gift cards are for gifts, not for payments.[3]
- If someone calls you and demands payment with gift cards, you know it is a scam. No exceptions!
- The scammers threatening you over the phone are likely too far away to hurt you. And even if they could, it's easier to call the next potential victim rather than send a thug to hurt you.

HANG UP!
The FBI
NEVER CALLS
YOU!

The truth is . . .

- Federal investigators are not going to tell you about upcoming drug arrests.
- Federal agencies such as the IRS, FBI, and CIA typically communicate through mail correspondence or in-person visits. It's rare for them to call people.

Strategies Scammers Use

SCAM
TRAP DOOR

#1 Scammers lure you in with a prize or a threat.

Here's what they'll say . . .

"You won a prize! Just give us your bank account number, and we'll deposit $10,000!"

Here are the facts . . .

No one makes a living giving away money. If someone offers you "free money," they are probably trying to scam you. Besides, with all the warnings Jesus makes about the dangers of wealth, who wants to take the spiritual risk of accepting a big chunk of money they didn't earn?[4]

☞ ***Here's what you must do:*** **HANG UP.**

BANK
SCAM
"BANK"

#2 Scammers pretend to be from an organization you trust.

Here's what they'll say . . .

"Hello, we are from the Townville Bank. We noticed some unusual activity on your account and would like you to confirm your name and account number."

Here are the facts . . .

Your bank already knows your name and account number. If you know and trust an organization, you can easily find their phone number. If you don't know it, find a friend who does. Call the number you trust to deal with the issue. If possible, visit your local bank branch to speak with a real person. Many times if you "confirm" your identity, it will start much more unusual activity.

☞ Say, ***"I'll call the number on my bank statement. Good-bye."*** THEN **HANG UP.**

SCAM
SCAM

#3 Scammers require payment with specific payment types.

Here's what they'll say . . .

"You need to withdraw your cash from the bank, place it in a box, go to the gas station at Prince and Lime Street, drop it in the open window of the red pickup, and walk into the store as if nothing is unusual. Or if it's easier, you can just ship it UPS."

Here are the facts . . .

Scammers like untraceable payment methods. Investigators can easily trace bank and credit card transactions. Payment methods like cash, gift cards, and cryptocurrency are usually untraceable.

☞ ***Here's what you must do:*** **HANG UP.**

SCAM
ACT NOW!

#4 Scammers pressure you to act immediately.

Here's what they'll say . . .

"If you do not claim the prize now, we have other people who will take it."

Here are the facts . . .

If it's really your money, you can get it on your schedule. If you have to hurry, you have to worry, and Jesus told us not to do that.[5] If someone else might get the prize, so what! They might need it more than you. It's selfish to think we need all the prizes, and besides, there usually isn't a prize anyway.

☞ ***Here's what you must do:*** **HANG UP.**

Fraud Prevention Steps

REGISTER DO NOT CALL LIST
DON'T BELIEVE CALLER ID

Fortify your phones.

Always be cautious about believing your caller ID. Scammers can make your caller ID display any name or number, and they can call from almost any country in the world.

Register your number with the National Do Not Call Registry. The process is simple and takes less than two minutes. Call 1-888-382-1222 and follow the prompts.

SCAM

If too many calls keep coming, change your phone number and only give that number to people who really need it. It's a small hassle that will eliminate lots of annoying phone calls.

Your local telephone provider may offer a screening option that reduces unwanted calls.

SCAM
NO

Get a second opinion.

We often get second opinions on healthcare decisions, and we should do the same with our money decisions. Choose a money partner with whom you discuss unfamiliar financial transactions or any decision that you are not quite sure about. For many people, it's a spouse, adult child, parents, an adult niece or nephew, church leader, or accountant. Don't ever be tricked into **not being allowed to talk** to someone about a financial situation. It's your money, not theirs. Remember, "In the multitude of counsellors there is safety."[6]

Birthdate
Social Security number
Credit Card number
SCAM
MY INFO IS PROTECTED
MY INFO

Guard your information.

Scammers are skilled at extracting key pieces of personal information, then using it to open bank accounts, loans, or credit cards in your name. You should never give the following information over the phone unless you have initiated the call or found the phone number on a verifiable document like a bank statement, business card, or other trustworthy source.

- birthdate
- Social Security number
- bank account number
- credit card numbers
- passwords
- online account information or other passcodes

SCAM
I have an
answer for
THAT!

Prepare standard responses.

What will you do?

- If an unrecognized number calls, the safest response is to let them leave a message and then call back if it is valid.
- If a caller supposedly from the IRS calls demanding payment, say, "I will have my accountant contact you about this." **Then hang up** and talk to your accountant.
- If pressured to buy something, say, "Let me think about it for a few days and discuss this with someone else." **Then hang up.**

JUST
HANG UP!

- If you receive a call from a family member who claims to be in trouble and needs cash, your credit card number, gift cards, or a money transfer, hang up. Call the phone number you have on record for them to see if they really need help.
- If a caller says, "Don't tell anyone," hang up, then tell someone right away.
- Realize it could happen to you.

People who assume they are too smart to get scammed, get scammed! Yes, it can happen to you!

Remember, gift cards are for gifts, not for payments!

What To Do If You Have Been Scammed

What To Do If You Have Been Scammed

Fraud victims often feel trapped and ashamed. They may blame themselves, replay the events, and agonize over missed red flags. These emotions can leave them susceptible to further scams.

1. Contact someone you trust and explain what happened.
2. If you gave a scammer a credit card or bank account number, then call your credit card company or bank, tell them what happened, and ask them about closing the account.
3. If you paid a scammer with gift cards, contact the place you purchased them and ask for help.

FEDERAL TRADE COMMISSION
ReportFraud.ftc.gov
FAQs
Update Report
Languages
Español
Report Now
Servicemembers, veterans, and military families: Report here.
Report to help fight fraud!
Report Now
Protect your community by reporting fraud, scams, and bad business practices.
REDIAL
FLASH

4. Consider using these government resources.

    a. Phone: Report a scam or identity theft at 1-877-382-4357 (1-800-FTC-HELP).

    b. Internet

        i. Report identity theft and get a recovery plan at www.identitytheft.gov.

        ii. Report a scam at www.reportfraud.ftc.gov.

5. Share your story.

Scammers are constantly changing their methods. If we share our stories, others can learn from our mistakes. It can be very embarrassing, but you may save someone the pain you went through.

Several fraud victims have agreed to share their stories which can be heard on Fraud Aware's *Listen Library.*

Call 717-562-0872 and follow the prompts.

Notes and Resources

Should we even buy gift cards to give as gifts?

Here's another way scammers use gift cards to steal money from people. They remove gift cards from stores, alter them, then secretly return them to the display area. When the gift card is purchased, the money is instantly transferred to the scammer.

You can protect yourself from this scam in several ways:

1. Only buy gift cards that are held in a locked case or that are stored behind a sales counter until they are purchased.
2. Do not buy gift cards with smudges, extra stickers, or worn edges.
3. Use gift cards as soon as practical after you receive them.
4. Consider not giving gift cards for substantial gifts. You can always give cash or write a check.

Is it rude to hang up the phone on scammers and telemarketers?

Is it rude to lock your door to keep a thief out? Hanging up on a scammer is no different. They are trained to manipulate you into staying on the phone so they can steal from you. There is no way you can win against a scammer. Be respectful, but we feel it's not rude to hang up the phone. In addition, hanging up will stop the conversation before you become angry and begin to act in non-Christian ways. It's a way out of temptation.

Telemarketers and scammers are real people with an eternal destiny. Jesus loves scammers and desires that they repent just like all of us. Instead of taunting or aggravating them, you could ask, "Is there any way I can pray for you?" If not, then hang up.

May you hang up on a telemarketer from a real company? Again, we feel it's not rude since some telemarketers are not allowed by their employers to hang up, until the person they called hangs up. By trying to be polite to them, you are wasting your time and theirs. Be courteous, but hang up.

Is this story true?

The names and details of this story are completely fictitious but represent a typical imposter fraud scheme where gift cards were used to extract money from a victim. Unfortunately, this problem is growing, and scammers are constantly developing new techniques. May you apply the principles in this book to live wisely.

Fraud Aware is a conservative Anabaptist 501(c)(3) committed to raising awareness about fraud and scams in our communities. Please contact us to receive free literature packets or to support our work.

We welcome feedback on this publication.

Fraud AWARE

Phone or Text (717) 740-2790 • PO Box 34, Ephrata, PA 17522
Fax: (717) 222-5266 • Web: FraudAware.us • Email: info@FraudAware.us

The Village That Burned $3 Million also by Davin Martin

Unfortunately, another village is preparing to burn another $3 million. *Can they be stopped?*

Using simple language, this parable exposes the development and consequences of illegal investment pools. The book also provides steps you can take to safeguard yourself and your community.

Order additional copies from:

CHRISTIAN LIGHT
PUBLICATIONS

Website: christianlight.org
Phone: 800-776-0478
Fax: 540-433-8896
Mail: PO Box 1212
Harrisonburg, VA 22803
Email: orders@christianlight.org

Discount available for bookstores.

About the Author

Davin Martin and his wife Katelyn live in Ephrata, Pennsylvania with their five boys. He has taught school for fifteen years, most of that full time. He now teaches part time, runs a small farm, and writes on the side. His first book *Foundations in Stewardship* was published by Weaverland Financial Aid.

Author's acknowledgments

- The Fraud Aware board—thank you for the time and energy you are investing in our communities through this work.
- An unknown caller fifteen years ago—thank you for helping me see my vulnerability to scams and motivating me to write by slickering me out of $35.

Foundations in Stewardship also by Davin Martin

Foundations in Stewardship offers 30 lessons weaving together practical financial advice, Biblical wisdom, and true stories. The lessons are targeted to conservative Anabaptist students in 8th or 9th grades. The course intends to shape students' vision and actions in the years before they begin earning and spending.

Five Themes in the Course

1. A steward's mentality recognizes God's ultimate ownership of everything, while an owner's mentality selfishly claims ownership of what he's been given.
2. A truly successful life is one of faithful stewardship, not accumulation of wealth.
3. Financial matters and spiritual matters directly impact each other and cannot be separated.
4. Wise stewards seek counsel from God, parents, and the church brotherhood.
5. The financial choices of youth will have lifelong consequences.

Student Workbook pictured.
Teacher's Guide with answers and lesson plans also available.

To purchase, contact

Home Messenger Bookstore
298 Wheat Ridge Drive
Ephrata, PA 17522
Phone 717-833-4456

Or
Christian Learning Resource
www.christianlearning.org

Fraud Aware believes that ***Foundations in Stewardship*** is a helpful resource for those seeking more financial teaching.

End Notes

1. Fraud Losses tab, All Quarters 2023. https://public.tableau.com/app/profile/federal.trade.commission/viz/FraudReports/FraudFacts, *accessed 3/22/24.*
2. John 8:32 "And ye shall know the truth, and the truth shall make you free."
3. https://www.ftc.gov/media/70967, *accessed 8/6/24.*
4. Matthew 13:22 "He also that received seed among the thorns is he that heareth the word; and the care of this world, and the deceitfulness of riches, choke the word, and he becometh unfruitful."
5. Matthew 6:34 "Take therefore no thought for the morrow: for the morrow shall take thought for the things of itself. Sufficient unto the day is the evil thereof."
6. Proverbs 11:14 "Where no counsel is, the people fall: but in the multitude of counsellors there is safety."